The Elephant in the Room

Poems by people with memory loss in Cambridgeshire

Edited and introduced by John Killick

Illustrated by Jo Chapman

Cambridgeshire Libraries

© Cambridgeshire Libraries on behalf of the authors,
and John Killick and Jo Chapman. September 2009

Published by:
Cambridgeshire County Council, Cambridgeshire Libraries,
Archives and Information, Shire Hall, Cambridge CB3 0AP

Funded by:
Department of Health, Eastern Region, Dignity in Care Campaign

Distributed by:
Lynda Martin, Dryden House, St John's Street, Huntingdon,
Cambridgeshire PE29 3NU
Email: Lynda.Martin@cambridgeshire.gov.uk

British Library Cataloguing in Publication record is available.

ISBN 9781904452331

Layout designed by: Hilltop: 01728 860975
Printed by: b&h digital: 01480 434200

Contents

Foreword and acknowledgements

Libraries are all about words - making sure we have access to words that can inform, enlighten, amaze and inspire. These are the words, unlocked by our poet in residence, John Killick, of some of our people living in Cambridgeshire. From across the county we have a rich source of responses in poetry and prose from the remarkable people that have been part of this project, this is a small selection.

We have been privileged indeed to have John Killick working with people with memory loss in Cambridgeshire during 2009, funded by the Department of Health, Eastern Region, Dignity in Care Campaign. Our project proposal was jointly inspired by John's work elsewhere in the country, and the vision and aims of the Dignity in Care campaign. As the project has progressed we have learnt from John's experiences of meeting residents and staff in various care settings in Cambridgeshire. We now have a better understanding of the challenges of providing a rich and caring environment where individuals and their unique experiences are cherished. We hope, as a result of this project and the training that John has provided, to enable an enriched and sympathetic rapport and patience in communicating with people with memory loss.

We have grown in understanding throughout this project and we hope that as you read these poems you will also have many moments of reflection and insight.

Acknowledgements
I am grateful for the support of the Steering Group for the project: Maggie Brown, Jacqueline Wieczoreck, Brenda Mead from Cambridgeshire Libraries, Allan James from Cambridgeshire County Council Adult Social Care, Suan Goh from Cambridgeshire Celebrates Age Steering Group, Christina Rowland-Jones from Arts and Minds, Karen and Jim Downes from the Alzheimer's Society and Angie Glew and Louise Molina from the Department of Health, and of course John Killick, our Poet in Residence.

Special thanks to artist Jan Bilston who attends the Alzheimer's Society Art Classes facilitated by Alan Hudleston and Gill Fordham for the wonderful elephant book cover illustration, and to Jo Chapman, Artist in Residence for Wisbech Library, for the stunning line drawings that accompany the poems. Jo is funded as part of the Big Lottery Community Library Award to work with the community on public art for the refurbished Wisbech library.

Cambridgeshire County Council has supported the project in many ways, with the use of County Council libraries for poetry readings and training venues, and with the enthusiastic contribution from a range of staff in Libraries, Adult Support Services, Older People's Services, Press and Publicity, Arts and Literature Development. It has been a fine example of partnership working to achieve a memorable and successful legacy for contributors, and a change in perspective for all those taking part.

Participants
Alzheimer's Society Groups meeting in Arbury and Great Shelford.

Day Centres at Cherry Trees, Cambridge (Age Concern); Hilltop, Cambridge; Hunters Down Huntingdon and the Oasis Centre, Wisbech.

Denbigh Ward, Fulbourn Hospital.

Residential Homes: Bramley Court, Histon; Brook House, Cambridge; Glennfield, Wisbech; Hatley Court, Waterbeach; Paxton Hall, Little Paxton, Oaklands, Bottisham; Primrose Croft, Cambridge Primrose Hill, Huntingdon and Rheola, St Ives.

Karen and Jim Downes.

LYNDA MARTIN
Partnership Manager,
Cambridgeshire Libraries,
Cambridgeshire County Council.

Introduction

Dementia is, of course, 'the elephant in the room'. It looms increasingly large in our lives, and we are reluctant to acknowledge it. It occasions a whole range of emotions in all of us. I hope that reading these poems will do something to dispel the stigma that swirls round the subject. The liveliness, honesty, courage and humour displayed here surely establish beyond doubt that there is life and creativity after diagnosis.

I should explain the process by which the poems came about. In a collaboration between poet and each person with the condition the words are written down or tape-recorded and then transcribed and subsequently shaped by me into a poem. They are then approved by the person and permission is given for publication; in some instances that authorisation comes from a relative. The most unbreakable rule is that I add nothing to a person's words, only select from the material given me. Sometimes no editing is necessary.

The grant which made this book possible came from a prize awarded by the Department of Health, Eastern Region as part of the national 'Dignity in Care' strategy. The project was managed by Cambridgeshire Libraries, and I worked over a period of 25 days in nursing homes, day centres and a hospital ward. The statistics are impressive: 77 individuals produced 67 poems and about a dozen pieces of prose. The enthusiasm and concentration of the participants was remarkable by any standards.

I should like to thank Louise Molina and Angela Glew of Department of Health, Eastern Region for their support, and Lynda Martin, Partnership Manager of Cambridgeshire Libraries, and her staff for providing the kind of organizational back-up a writer can only dream of. But most of all I want to pay tribute to the people with dementia themselves, and their family and staff supporters, who have carried this residency along on a tide of goodwill and expectancy. I hope they feel rewarded by this publication.

JOHN KILLICK
Poet in Residence

On Words

Words are so important,
especially if they're the right ones.
They're so important — I must think!

I remember words my mother used
when I was very much younger.
They come back to me in my thoughts
because she was very wise,
has always been, and still is.

One doesn't always think about the words —
they just trot out in the middle of a sentence.

People use words
that don't really apply to the situation.
They don't mean
what the person thinks they mean.
'If in doubt say nowt'
— that's a good defensive puzzle
but this is the way
the world's beginning to think!

I sometimes wonder
'Who am I to say this?'

I wonder if other people
feel the same way about words,
or if they do not?

Evelyn Hodgson

On Music

Life is about all sorts of things.
I have a degree in music and in philosophy,
both of which are really interesting things,
the one is as interesting as the other.

When I first started to play the piano
the people who gave me lessons —
I gave them up because it wasn't
giving me what I needed.

I went to somebody else because
they were much better – you have to have
something personal coming out of it –
'This is me, this is me, this is my sound.'

If music is a language like food:
as far as I'm concerned I enjoy it very much,
I'm very particular about what I eat,
the things you put in your throat.

And I've gone on with all these people,
the ones in this area,
at first I would take it
but now it's 'Take it away!'

If music is like a garden:
a beautiful garden is put closely together,
taken care of, a thing of retrieval,
and music is trying that too,

but the way it is played is perhaps not,
you can build it up as you go,
you can stand up and sing with it –
it's a question of feeling, of hearing, of saying 'YES!'

Raymond Cook

Drumming

I'm the real person.
I'm right for living.
I liked to listen to music and singing.
I knew at school I could sing,
but I didn't know about the drumming.

When the modern thing was coming along
and getting favoured, I thought
'Oh, I'd love to do that!'
He was well-known locally
and said yes, he'd teach me.
He got me in a position
where I was comfortable
and knew I could play.

Dance-band to rock,
I don't mind either.
I always had the backing,
and good pay for it too.
There's so much more to it
than most people think.
As I went on with the drumming
the singing got better too.
I loved it so much
I'd have done it for nothing
but I never told them that.

Everyone has a time of life
when they think it's wonderful,
and that was it for me.

Clive Welham

Crocheting Man

It's the third year we've been coming here
and they hadn't got no cushions on the chairs.
I suggested I put out an appeal for wool
to make them some cushion covers.
I took on the challenge to do one
for each cushion we used, which was twelve,
and I made one cover a week.

I'd learned to crochet in 1979
on the caravan site. A lady
of turned 80 learned me to do it:
"Get some wool and a hook
and I'll show you how to start."
I did some little squares
and took it back and showed her
and she pulled it all down
and told me to do it properly.
She done that two or three times.
At the time we was running dance classes
for sequence dancing. When I started
crocheting I decided to make covers
for the plastic chairs people sat on.
I went from cushion covers to settee covers.
Then I went on to baby shawls.
Then I went on to blankets — six by five
for a double-size bed. I made one
for the caravan for the cold nights,
then one for our own bed at home.
And in between I made cot blankets.
Now I've even had the trouble
of teaching people to crochet while I've been here!

Women always have the wool in their left hand
and hook it round their left finger.
I have my wool in my right hand
and my hook, and I put the wool over
with my forefinger. I've got the women
saying "Ernie, aren't you quick!"

My uncle used to do embroidery.
I've tried cross-stitch but it takes time
before you see benefit from the labour.
I can just sit there crocheting
and watch television at the same time.

The greatest benefit that comes from it
is that it keeps your fingers nimble.
And the things people say –
they think it's marvellous that you do it!

Ernie Johnson

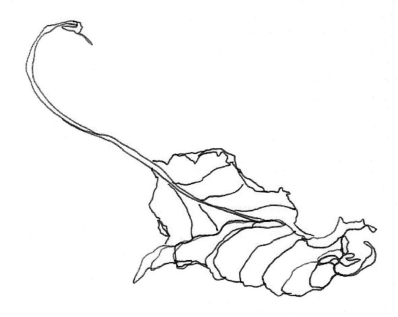

All That Jazz

Clacton was flattened
I went there with Linda
we used to go dancing
rock-and-roll stuff
I went in for Disco Champion
and won in 1970-something.

I like doing rock-and-roll
but I like listening to Dixieland —
George Melly, Kenny Ball,
Acker Bilk, Chris Barber
and further back Kid Ory
and I've got Louis Armstrong
I've heard them all,
all of that era.

I think it'll last for ever.
This modern stuff is all
a big axe and back to front!

Len Nolde

Edible Perfection

I was a cakemaker most of my life,
icing birthday cakes, anniversary cakes.
Many oohs and aahs dragged out
of people's mouths by the cakes I made.
People admired and buyed.
The qualities required
are the value of eyesight
and the application of the hand.

There is one cake that I made —
six-foot high in Royal Icing —
that produced many oohs and ahhs
of ecstatic value from hundreds of people.
It was a bit of a masterpiece
and I admit I was quite proud of it.
Fortunately, made in the proper manner,
the edible content of cakes remains
for months on end, their sell-by-date
is, shall we say, extensive.
So even that one was for consumption.
It is amazing that the aspiration
of this amazement emerged from one person.

Bob Wolffs

Life Below Stairs

After the Duke of Windsor abdicated
I was transferred to the Palace.
There were thirty-three housemaids there,
and I got lost every day. Every day!
They said "Turn left and then turn right…."
but I could never get it right — oh dear!

We made beds in the morning,
but before that we did the drawing-rooms
and the lounges. There were six of us.
They weren't dirty, but you did them.
You dusted them. They always used to say
"There's that little girl from the country —
she's making love to the furniture!"

I used furniture cream, and I was always
very particular. I used to think
'I wonder how many princes and kings
have sat on this chair. And I wonder
how many titled people have sat at that table?'

Before, when we were at Windsor,
Elizabeth and Margaret had to have cooking lessons,
and the kitchen was downstairs,
then they'd come up into my pantry.
They'd have pockets in their little aprons
where they'd put sugar-lumps they'd pinched.
They were kind of kiddy-like
but they loved their cooking!

When I came into service
there was a saying my mother told me:
'Manners Maketh Man'. And it's true.
You don't have to be well off
if you've got good manners.
Good manners will take you anywhere.

Amy Christina Allum

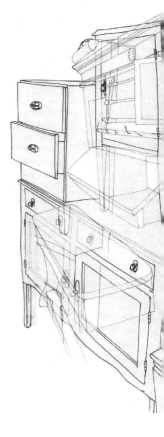

On Aran

At times I've gone across
over to the Aran Islands
but not commonly.
I don't come from there.

My brother goes out there
— he's a big man anyway.
He's very taken with them,
so he goes back often.

I think it may have been
my brother taking me
in a boat — he's competent —
a strong, strong man.

Once you're out there
I know it really well.
It's a chilly place
but I have a warm feeling about it.

The people are good, but
during the day they somehow slip away.
They've gone, have other places to go to,
but they're still there, they still belong.

The way of life can be attractive
but in a simple way.
It's good in its rights now.
It'll stay. They can do it.

Up to a point
but not all of the time
the scenes come back to me
strongly and with great pleasure.

Patrick Brenchley

Fascinated By Foliage

Look at it out there –
have you ever seen anything like it?
It's this all the way in –
you go in and you come out.
The first time I went into it
I thought 'I could die here!'
You've got to admit it's lovely.
I wake up every morning
and I look out and I think
this whole place is fantastic!

Have you seen that foliage there?
Just turn around and look.
As far as the eye can see
I love every bit of it.
It wasn't always like that.
When I first came I thought
they look so weird, those things,
you know, those things dangling down.
I used to get really fanky.

My husband said "Those are trees!"
I said "Well I'll have to go somewhere else!"
But it's a long time ago,
and now I think they're outstanding.
They're not just trees, are they?
They're different. I know it's odd –
look how high it is, and
the way they come down from the top
instead of up from the ground.

When I first came I'd say
"Come and look at these things!"
And he'd say "Have a look down here".
And I'd say "I'm not interested in down there,
it's all sticks and dead things. It's them –
I don't want them in my garden!"
But I got used to it. They're wonderful.

I think they're just fascinating.
I've been mesmerised with them
ever since we moved here.

Veronica Watts

Horses And Me

This is telling the truth
of what I feel for the horse
and what comes out of me
into the horse, and what comes back
from the horse into me.
It works both ways. We're both
giving and taking from one another.
And it's a good sign.
It's what you feel,
it's what you feel in the game.

This is the way I feel about it
and the way I feel about the horse
as well as myself. It's not just me
I'm worried about, it's the horse as well.
I'm worried about both of us.
So we go as a team,
and that's how it should be,
it should be as a team.
That's the way I treat the horse,
as a team to me,
and I'm a team to them.

I prefer horses
to a lot of human beings
because I get more satisfaction
out of a horse than I get
out of these human beings.
I trust the horse.

It's just amazing --
well I feel I'm just ordinary,
living and growing up
and growing old.

I want to grow old with my horses.
They show me the way to go home.

George Green

Sudden Blindness

I knitted and sewed and crocheted
and drawed and everything
and went to bed one night perfect
and when I woke up — nothing!
I said to my husband "I can't see!"
He said "Don't start so early."
It was a terrible shock.
What caused it they never knew.
They said it might come back,
but that was seven years ago.

Your eyes are precious to you.
Look after them whatever you do.
I hope every day.
But somebody's worse than me,
that's what I say

Joan Howard

My Birds

The swans at Welney come down
from the frozen wastes where they breed.
They come from Iceland,
they fly a long way.
I go to look at them specially each year,
I take a lot of photographs.
There are special kinds:
the Hooper swans from Iceland
and the Bewicks —
they come from England,
they're rough ones, nasty ones,
they beat up other swans.

Then there's woodpeckers:
the green ones, the little ones too.
This is the sort of time when they look out for nests.
They drum along the trunks to make holes.
The green ones have a red crown,
but as they go into the breeding season the colours fade.

Goldfinches are very pretty, some people would say,
but I wouldn't — I don't want to call them pretty,
It's fine to see them without naming them.
Some people have a birdbasket in their garden,
I'd have one myself
but in the flats where I live they don't like it —
the droppings from the birds might attract rats.

I think the way birds come
and are quite independent
and are a part of nature
is why I really like them.

Brian Ratcliffe

The Qualities Of Kite-ing

You can get two people who are kiters
and then the conversation starts to flow.
We always used to travel around the country,
and the continent, of course.
The friends you meet are terrific –
you go out three, four, five, six,
and from there get attached to others
till you make a quorum,
and the kites go up high
and then they come down again.

There's the size of kites –
Butterflies for the babies
and all the variants along the scale
up to the big Flare kites,
they fly with two hands.
They are ones that can do a lot of damage –
to yourself as well.

It's a funny excitement flying a kite –
it doesn't do what you want it to do
until you've got it under control.
You're upset at first at not being in charge.
The wind is fighting you at that stage
then it's elation when you gain control.
When the kite overcomes the wind
it's "Get up there!" and it keeps
up there all day if you want.

It's a fight between you and the kite.
This is the challenge you are throwing out.
Once you can control the kite
you can make it do what you want,
but once one part goes wrong
you lose it – see little Johnny running along
to the Pierhead trying to catch it!

If someone's flying a kite too near you
it takes the air-waves away from you,
it's juggling about with the atmosphere.

You have to lie back on the wind
to get more pressure on the face of the kite.
If the wind was strong enough
to hold the kite horizontal
it might lift the kite up
and you with it – it's a one-in
one-out, one-in one-out job.

The material is plastic, the line is cord.
The variants of colour is so great
that it's unbelievable really,
it's just a thrill. Peg it in the ground
and leave it there if it's a good wind.

We don't start flying till four o'clock!

William George Elder

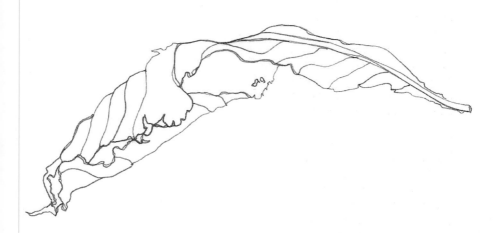

Being Here

I'm relatively new here.
I was diagnosed with Early Onset Alzheimer's
only three or four weeks ago.
It started off with an occupational health referral
and then an MRI scan
and it all went on from there.
Once they get you in on one thing
they get you on another
further down the line.

I worked as an administrator
at Anglia Ruskin University
but now I'm unemployed.
Once you are diagnosed
you have to write to the DVLA
and now I can't drive.

I quite enjoy being here.
I just come once a week.
Everyone is very nice.
I don't feel labelled
and it doesn't make any difference
to friends or family.
And I haven't noticed any difference.

To others, depending on the diagnosis, I say:
surround yourself with those you get on with,
and help those around you who need help.

To myself, I say:
keep on breathing, Barbara!

Barbara Cridland

Twins Together

People say we're not the least alike —
I'm like Mum, she's like dad.
She never used to be as tall as me.
I wish she'd have been here with me now.
We've just been together all the time.

She was terrified of the school and everything.
It's me that used to go and punch the boys
to get them to leave her alone.
It's those boys that are half-daft.
Part of her used to make me angry
and those that were teasing her made me angry —
that's a double anger I was feeling —
what they wanted was a damn good hiding!
Some of the teachers used to be nasty too.
I said to Jean "You know what I'm going to do
when I get out?" but I never did.
But I'm proud of myself I stood up for her.

Now it's funny really, when we go out,
I'm always looking for things
and *she's* saying "Don't be daft!"

Joan Allen

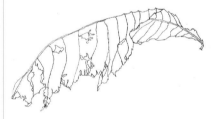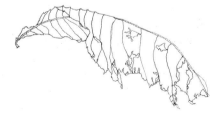

No Place Like Home

Think Canada think cold:
in the winter that's what it is,
but in the summer where I was
it got so hot and humid
you could be sitting chatting
with the sweat rolling off you!

But I did go camping one weekend
in Algonquin National Park.
We canoed and found you get
lots of mosquitoes in the summer.
We used to get up really early
and set off while the lake was calm
because the wind gets up later on.
We had a flat bottom canoe
which is said to be more stable.
The birchbarks are quicker
but they are for the experts.
It is a vast and forested place:
Man hasn't really encroached it.
There they talk about 'my cottage',
which is their place by the lake,
whereas here they say 'my place at the beach'.

I lived in London, Ontario
but I couldn't stand the climate.
I was born in King's Lynn
and now I live in Wisbech.
A friend from Norfolk said
"We're a pair of old Swedes,
or a pair of Norfolk dumplings!"

Marie Youngman

Trouble At T'mill

I was born a Romany
and lived in a caravan
you see different places
me dad used to make clothes-pegs
me mam went around the 'ouses selling 'em
me brother worked in t'pits
and I worked in t'cotton factories

I worked wi me sister
and one day me 'and was in t'way
when she turned t'machine on.
I shouted "Turn that bloody machine off!"
She asked "What's t'matter?"
I yelled "Look at me fingers!"
I 'it 'er and got t'sack.

I went back next day
T'boss said "I thought I'd sacked you!"
I said "Me sister did it."
'E said "You're only little
but you're an awkward bugger."
When I got 'ome me dad said
"'Ow did yer get on terday?"
I said "I'm goin' ter kill 'er!"

I couldn't get on wi' 'er.
She thought she were better'n me —
she were one o' them!

Susannah Hanson

A Teacher's Life

It was a long time ago.
I need some notes to help me.
I've almost forgotten,
but not completely.

I was a teacher for at least forty years.
I was at one school all the time.
When I retired I was Deputy Head.
I was never actually a full one because
I enjoyed the teaching so much,
staying in the actual classroom.
And I had a lot of extras to do as well –
things that I enjoyed.

I liked being with the children
and getting them to know different things.
We had a few naughty children.
I used to put them to one side
and give them something different to do.
The most difficult were the slower ones.
I had, first of all, to find
different ways of getting them interested.
The staff I had at the time
were pretty good at helping as well.
They could think of such interesting ways,
which helped me greatly, of course.

We were quite a big school –
it must have been round here,
but not immediately, but in this area.
On the whole we had supportive parents
but we did have a few difficult ones –
I suppose really they are the most difficult to do.
We had quite a little group at one time
of children who were difficult.
Some of the staff I had were very keen
in helping the children in the holiday times.

I had had lots of holidays,
going there and there and there,
and by the time I'd finished
I'd been just about everywhere
that I wanted to go, really.

The last lot that I had
were very nice children.
There weren't many difficult ones.
It made a good finish for me.
I was very lucky –
I went out on a high note.

I went to train at…. where?
Homerton College, Cambridge –
see, I remembered!
My dear dear college,
We were all so happy there!
I must have taken an exam,
I must have delivered something.
I'll have to make time
for a little walk there.

Homerton College, Cambridge –
I haven't been back, or
reading about it, or anything,
and there it came –
straight out of my head!

Mary Gadsby

Good Friends

When I was younger I had a lot of very nice people
around and helping –
Mary, Lou and Phil.
Then I started to grow up
and that changed things a bit.

I suppose sometimes in my brain I thought
they were really good friends to me
and that they were really good friends to others.

I was very fond of them –
Mary, Lou and Phil –
but I was a bit timid.
I didn't know whether I could deliver,
but I didn't want to lose them.
But everyone grows up, don't they?

Nobody is tiptop well
unless they are tiptop lucky.
Getting older is one of the problems for me
I put my feet up
and say "Well, I've done a lot already."
A lot of people don't want to listen
to other people's problems,
and the others who helped me
are less alive now.

You walk and you do what you do
and suddenly the memories come up and hit you –
Mary, Lou and Phil –
they were so nice to me then
and I wasn't so nice to them.
I haven't forgotten,
and I feel guilty.

Christine Lyall Grant

Walking In Toft

I like walking
I do a walk every day.
We live in the countryside
and on three sides there's trees,
all through the garden and beyond.
Even in the garden there's nothing but growth.

There's one that we do more than any other.
It's the correct length.
It varies. You go up and down —
the countryside undulates
and the views are the same all around.

(I say we — it's my husband and I
— we're fortunately still together.)

Immediately we go through a bushy bit
that's not supposed to be an opening but is.
Then we turn onto the beginning of a lane
and just follow that for half-a-mile
and it just goes on and on into the countryside.

Occasionally we meet somebody.
There's somewhere a couple of men
have an allotment and grow things.
We chat with them.

You retrace your steps to some extent.
It's the Toft Wood that we walk through.
No views at all. It's not a very big wood
but full of lovely trees.

We haven't been here long.
We're settling into the landscape.

Beryl Hallett

Skating

I did all the things you can do in a village.
In the wintertime I ended up skating,
and skating was a major thing in Upwell,
because the river ran right through the centre.
If we had any frost at all it would freeze
and you could go on the river for miles —
near to Ely one way, and the other way
right through the Middle Level System —
they reckoned you could go twenty-six miles.
They even skated at midnight.
I skated from five to sixteen.

The only reason that you can't skate
is that you haven't got a chair.
If you've got a chair you can use it
to support you while you skate
to start you off. Any child (a four or five-year-old)
would put on the skates — the Fen-Runner
and the Dutch-Runner were the two types there were.
The Dutch-Runner was a flat blade about
a quarter-inch wide which you stood on —
it's a dead flat blade. But the Fen-Runner,
which was the local one, has a curb
at the end, so you can't hurt yourself,
for the simple reason that if you veer to the side
of the river it just rides up and protects you.

You've probably got five or six weeks
of every year when you can go skating.
You can't do it now because the climate's changed
and the places we used to skate have changed,
because all that skating was done on Cobit Wash
and that wasn't actually the river, it was
flooded land. It's now got so usable
it's mostly been ploughed. The last five years
they've had an attempt to run the amateur programme.

Skating is really exhilarating. As soon
as I came out of school I'd be on the skates.
All day and all night too,
if you could, you'd be on the skates.
I suppose nowadays there'd be thousands
of reasons of safety not to allow the children on.
But not then. On the other hand,
it built your confidence up in what you could do.
Once you could skate you were set up for life.

John Garner

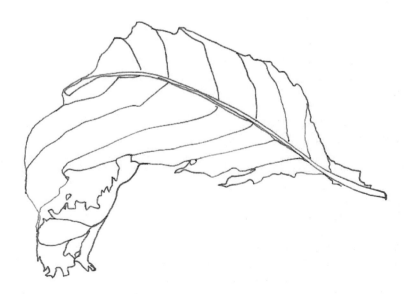

Laugh And Enjoy

I'm as daft as a brush.
Most things, they make me laugh,
I can giggle all day.

It's a pleasant little place round this corner.
I never knew there were so many trees out there.
They're blowing about a lot today.

My role is a mother with children,
all looking very good.
And they say to me "Can we go? Can we go?"
And I say "Yes, and don't be late!"

From time to time I go with a friend
to cater for more than anything
and get the ladies cling together
at the time and get the stories going.
It's to do with the Church.

Out there my hair will blow about —
there'll be nothing left of it,
I'll be as bald as a baby!

I don't go down the pub.
They'd say "Look at her, drinking!"
But I'd say "I will do what I want to do!"

I like looking after the family,
then off to do the shopping.
But it's "I want! I want!"
But I say "You'll get what I give you!"

"Let's go on a picnic" —
this was in times of sunshine.
Hopefully they'll come again.

Look at those trees —

the branches are blowing everywhere,
I'm surprised they haven't broken.

Crikey, this is going back all those years.
I can still look at the clothes I wore —
they're posh, really posh —
that's the only word I can come up with.
I used to put them on —
I honestly thought I was going to fail myself.

Very often I'm singing,
singing when I least expect it,
and I think 'What have I done?'
But whenever there's a party going on in our street
it's "Will you do the singing?"

Now I miss out on a lot of things really,
but it makes you feel proud
when you do things for yourself.

Veronica Bowen

Incident At Selwyn

It wasn't the job I wanted.
It wasn't my sort of work.
I only went there as a temporary
and stayed twenty-four years.
I would clean and look after them.
I used to meet all kinds of students.

I remember one especially:
he tried to commit suicide.
I didn't know what to do —
whether to sort him out
or get to the phone.
I think it was the exams —
they were too much for him.
He would get muddled over things:
he couldn't decide to do one thing
or to do something else.
I would sit ages with him.
He did go away after
but came back to see me.
He said "You saved my life."

Afterwards there was always
a lot choosing my rooms.

Dorothy Pearson

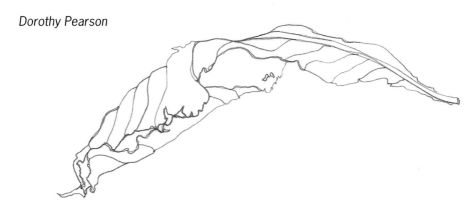

Funny Days At The Palace

My mother was rather strict
and I was glad to get away.
I decided I'd go to London.
One of my sisters went as well.
We took jobs at the Palace.
We lived in down under,
and moved in with the others.
We had some funny days there.

You said hello to the men
who were knocking up the coals.
You did anything anyone told you –
"Bring me this" and "Bring me that" –
you were running all over the Palace.
There was Head Butler to Footman.
You never touched the Head Butler –
he gave all the orders.
If he wanted a chair moved
you never argued, you moved it.
We often made mistakes
but nobody ever noticed.
If you didn't want to meet them
you went in the first door,
waited till they'd gone,
and then popped out again.
We had some good laughs:
the way the young ones dashed along corridors;
the way the Footman cleaned a table –
he'd polish the surface with his socks
as if brushing the snow away.
Then we'd dance on the table.......
And nobody knew it but us!

Audrey Maffey

It's My Life

Once upon a time
I'd have said no, I can't do that,
but now I've grown up.

A part of me wants to find
what my husband is doing.
The moment I see him come home
I want to live.

The hot weather?
Take it outside
and melt it quick!

One day I might be strolling somewhere
holding a little bag again……

This book you're writing in –
it's just the right size
and the right shape for everything.
The only time I shall ever know
is when it suddenly decides
to be writing there for me.

I'm a bit more than seventy.
How much? This is the slowest bit.
I can never get that far.
My Golden Wedding,
that will be the next one.
We're creeping upwards gradually.

You look very puzzled.
I've left you out so long,
but at least you're honest!

Life is quite fun,
if you can make it so.
It's my life, that's certainly true.

It's been interesting, the whole thing.
Now I can just get up
and go where I like.

Daisy Miller

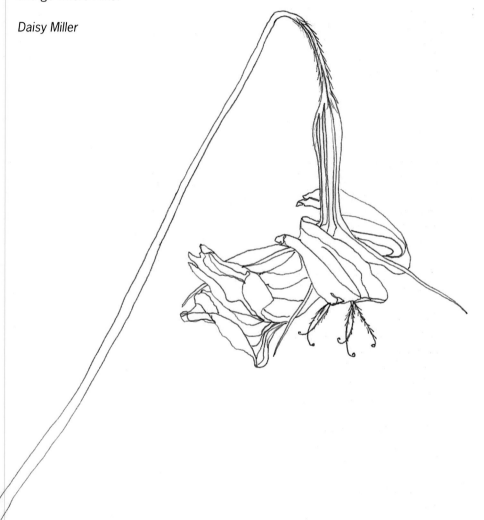

Stranger Here

I'm a nosey parker,
getting interested in things I shouldn't.
I pick them up,
open them out,
and put them back again.

I hear things.
I think they're good
or they're not good.
I don't pass them on,
I leave them to themselves.

I lost my gold ring —
it fell down the drain
and I couldn't get it back.

I lost my handbag —
it fell in the river
but I didn't tell anyone.

Edgbaston I was born —
we called it 'Heads Bashed In'! —
a very posh part of Birmingham.

I did catering and jumble sales
but I don't know round here.
Where I was brought up
I knew the rounds.

I liked life,
and I still do,
but I don't feel comfortable
because I don't come from here.
Now I'm too old
to start again from the bottom.

Iris Lilian Hems

Conversation

People are so different.
Everyone is different.
You have to keep yourself back a little
to see what they're like
before you can talk easily.

Where people are withdrawn
you keep asking them things
so that they have to reply.
Most people like to talk
but they're afraid to talk,
they're afraid they might be boring,
so you have to make it clear
you are interested in them.

Where people are stuck in one direction
I listen for as long as I can bear it
then I say "Could I just mention that....?"
and sometimes this works.

Where you can't stand a person
you can't ignore people
But you get away as quickly as you can.

Some people are very clever
at ignoring you, or turning away
and not listening to you.
I usually say "Tell me what you think
about so-and-so", and that lets them
get it out of their system.

One thing can lead to another
and sometimes you wish you'd never started.
But it makes it much more interesting
if it goes somewhere you haven't expected.

Angela Wheeler

Statement

I like to test myself out.
The point is that with the dementia
I lose the words. I can get them,
but it takes time.

I've found that the most important thing
is to have people who are on your side,
on the same side of the house.

You have to be very careful
when you're dealing with someone with dementia.
It's something which on the surface seems so simple,
but underneath can reveal all sorts of horrors.
You have to consider the person you're dealing with.

And this can happen, I have found, so easily:
it's happening to many in here —
they can't understand what's happening to them;
they can't understand why they can't go out;
they can't understand why they have a room number.

It was said to me today
"When you've nothing to do
and all day to do it in….."
I'm still perplexed by it, to some extent.
But it's true: I return to my room
and bang my brains about.

Peter Hollingsworth

The Split

When I was diagnosed
it was just a matter of telling me I'd got it
and leaving me to get on with it

Jim and I kept it to ourselves at first.
We were both crying –
it's a big thing to come to terms with.

My younger sister and my mother
asked me to say I had cancer
because mentally I would bring shame on the family.

I just can't understand why a mother
would want to have a daughter with cancer
rather than Alzheimer's.

We're a split family –
dementia has split our family –
and there's no way to heal it now.

Karen Downes

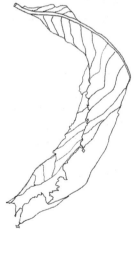

Comings And Goings

What I can't make out is
I wrote to Arthur Edwards
and never got no word whatsoever.

Then I wrote to my father
and I thought he'd come and see me
but he never came either.

I think they might have got fed up with me
I couldn't pick a fight
I don't suppose I would.

I don't know where father went in the morning
he just come in and must have got his coat
and I haven't seen him since.

You couldn't get things like Teddy during the War
so I keep him against me like this
and I won't ever let him go.

Grace Edwards

My Angering Thoughts

I get very angry about
that I have a brain inside but
I cannot say something and remember
what I said ten minutes later.
And I cannot remember
something someone has said ten minutes later.

Another of my angering thoughts
is this: is it because
I have this pernickety sort of mind
that I have developed this kind of dementia?

No longer 'Unsinkable'
now 'Demented of Duxford'!

Molly Brown

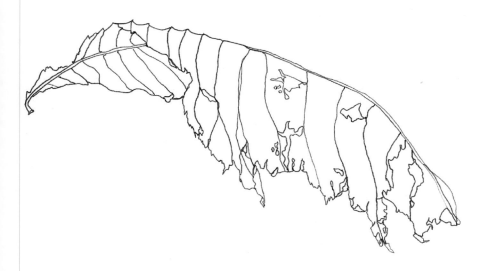

Miffed

I'm a bit miffed
that I've got this horrible thing.
I know there's nothing I can do about it
and that there's nothing you can do about it.

It takes me a long time to say things.
This is what happens:
as soon as I want to say something,
this happens….. and then I can't do it.

We used to look after children.
We had some fun
with the children that came:
there was one girl that came
and she was so naughty we loved her.

I knew exactly what I would do
when I retired – it was fostering.
And then I couldn't go down that road,
and that was such a shame.

'Why?' you wonder,
'What makes things like this happen?'
I say to myself
'Ok, you've got it.'
And I go to Church
and they're wonderful to me,
they look after me
and do things for me –
people are very kind, so kind.

I try not to look at the future.
I want to try to keep going
just as long as I can.

Sally Jane Pettit

Using My Brain

What I've done this year is a thinking process.
I'm now coming back to the land of questioning things.

It's important you think the right things
or you turn in upon yourself.
This is the phase when I need to be opening outwards.

Bryan Kingman

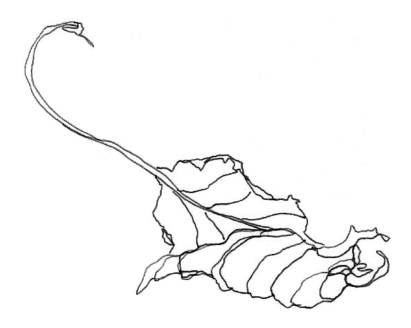

The Map

I take life as it comes.
If you look at nature
there's a pattern there —
the seasons and the flowers,
the trees and the grass.

But humans are not animals,
so you must have a map
or you don't know where you are.
I've a map in my mind.
I hope it's the right one.
It's essential to have one.
The problem is following it.
You pick up hints on the way
and others will give you hints.
Provided you take their pace
you'll be alright.
If you go too slow
that'll cause friction
because everyone has
this or that to do.

Of course our age helps —
you can't be in too much of a hurry.
because you have a belief
in yourself it's the right road
you keep it firmly
in your mind that it is.

You have to check your map
where you've got to
but not too often because
if you're too slow
you'll hold everything up.

It's a gift. You're given it.
It comes from above you.
It comes from the light.
It shows you the way.

John Parnell

On Track

I'm remembering the old Speedway.
It used to be the thing when I was younger.
I'm going back a bit here.
I played a slow-down version,
I gave it a run.
Speedway comes from a scoring situation,
I seemed to get that impression.
Over the years it's been really entertaining.
There used to be some fine riders.
Them that survived were pushing
their lives to make something of it.
Them as do go go for a reason,
and that's to enjoy themselves.

Dogtrack is the same area —
in one end of the stadium,
Speedway at the other.
Watching the dogs was
an evening's entertainment.
But we don't want
to get on the lager tour!

We all get on pretty well together.
There's not one, I think,
during the period I have been here,
have not enjoyed themselves.
You wouldn't, perhaps, feel at home
in the first instance —
you've stepped out into
an area that's different.
But the ladies'll keep me going!

I'm too clever for my bloody self!
Don't take me too seriously.
I know I'm on form,
but I was trying to tell you
too many things

and I've misled you.
But it's nice to be here,
stringing it out.

Jack Bell

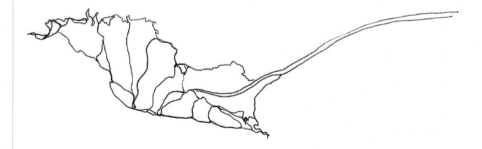

I Wonder Why

Do you think there's a place up there I can go to?
Or a place down there?
I just think you die and are buried
and that's the end of you.
The sky up there is just a lovely blue.

Mary Edwards

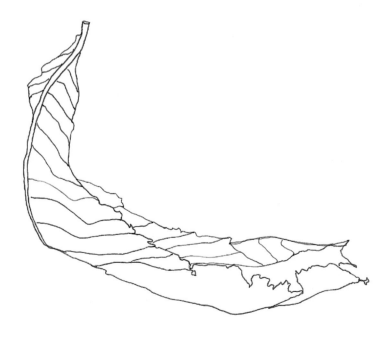

Half-way Irish

Irish? I'm half-way there.
It's really quite determined.
"You wouldn't know, would you now?"

In a sense Ireland's a place
with a good feel to itself
which it retains when it comes to England.

We like to come over.
It's quite a strong stand we make.
I hadn't come across it before.

I'm not the ideal person
to speak of England,
not perfect by any means.

Nearly a year back
me and my brother
went across the country

saying a few things
to give places identity.
We came to Cambridgeshire.

We know it's a good place in life.
We liked it and moved to it.
Now Cambridge is taking over.

Patrick Brenchley

The Travelling Butcher

I was born in Huddersfield.
I became a butcher —
an advert in the local paper.
I like nothing much about Yorkshire —
too cold and bleak.
I was pleased when the War broke out.
That's how I got away from it.
I said "I'm going to join up."
Best thing I ever did.
I never did settle down.

I've been to a lot of Stations.
And I can tell you they're all the same.
Only RAF — but I'm not rejoining.
Went to West Africa twice,
that's the furthest I was ever sent.
It was a bit noisy with mosquitoes.
'Unfit for Service in West Africa'.
But I was a butcher —
"Oh, we need you!"
So I was sent out again.
You see, all trades were wanted.
If we weren't there they couldn't fly.

Then there was Jersey.
"If you stay over ten years you get a pension."
So I stayed fifteen.

Then there was France.
Nice people the French.
Once you were in you were in,
but they had to get to know you properly.

I've been here six months without causing a row,
Not once saying "Let me out! Let me out!"
but I haven't got a word in it at all.
People always know more than you do.

I've been thinking: after all this —
I've been through hellfire and water —
what have I finished up with:
nothing. It's a crying shame!

Geoffrey Townend

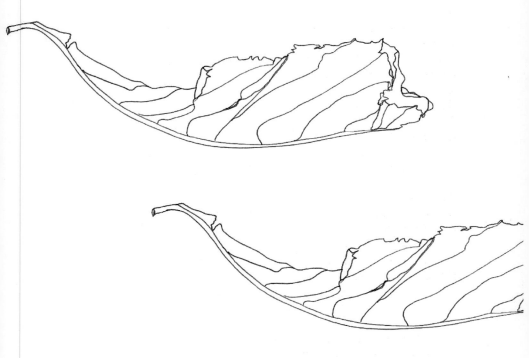

Handling The Dogs

I have trained 163 dogs this year.
They will not bite
anybody that's come from Scotland
right down to London.

I train the dog to be a dog.
The dog can't bite
if you train it right.
You can bring an alsation in here
now wanting to bite me,
and in two or three seconds
I'll have that dog at my feet
with its tail wagging.
Don't ask me how it's done,
but it's done.
I'm not brilliant,
but I know how to train dogs.

Keeping it to myself
is the only safe way to do
because if she knew
she would tell her friend
who would tell her friend
and before we knew
there'd be hundreds doing their own thing.
That would be the worst thing
that could happen because
the majority of people
would train their dog in their own way.
Who's going to follow my advice
and do as I tell them?
Not very many.
It's like an army sergeant.
He tells them what to do,
and they don't argue with him,
they just do what he says.
But it could be the wrong thing:

they could be dead,
they could be shot.
I don't tell anybody,
and I believe that only you
should be the one to train that dog.
I'll train every dog they give me
But I'll not have any people
knowing how I'm doing it.

The dogs will eventually
win their own war.
The tail will start wagging.
You watch a dog's tail:
if a dog comes up to you
and he's 'aargh aargh'
and you put your hand down
and he puts his nose to your hand,
what does he do?
He licks your hand.
Why? Your hand tastes of salt
and he will not attack salt.
Don't ask me why that's the law,
why the dog does that —
we just don't know.

The dog will not attack salt,
but make sure it doesn't go in the eyes.
You put it in the middle of your hand.
"Come on, son! Come on!"
He'll come up and smell it,
look at you, look at you again,
and the third time his tongue comes out
and he's licked the salt.
Why? We don't honestly know the truth.
We're telling you what happens.
Because if everybody knew
they'd be tricking the dogs into it.
These people all love animals.

I'm going to keep the secret.
There's two other people know.
That's all. You think
I've told you but I haven't.

William Craig

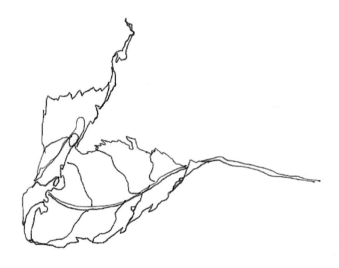

Racing As It Is

First thing in the morning
we start at half-six.
We come in and muck out.
We do our two-three stables and
we carry on and work through.
We get them ready to go out.
We can't be too slow, as you have
to make sure you get a break between.

When we get them out
we all shout for stop.
We get on the horses,
walk round in a big circle.
We follow one another.
There's one of the older ones
we call 'The Lead Horse'.
And the one at the back —
that's one that's a bit lazy
and won't lay up, so you've got
to have a lead for him.

Then we trot up and down.
Then we canter. One canter
at first, and it just depends
if it's a work day
or if it's an ordinary day.
If it's a work day
they go much faster and
they do more exercise
and more than one canter.

Then we start galloping them
as far as they have to go —
could be a mile,
could be a mile-and-a quarter,
could be a mile-and-a-half
or five or six furlongs.

Horses are different kettles of fish.
The horse takes it in itself
and when it's looking
you can see it's really keen.
It keeps trying, always trying
to do better than it did before.

We walk them back
after the work-outs
very slowly to the stables.
It's just a matter
of settling them down.
One minute they're stirred up
and the next still very jumpy.
It's taking everything
piece by piece, get the horse
when it's done enough
it eventually realizes
it knows it's going home,
that it's done for the day.

You take them in
and you wash them down.
If they're sweaty
you scrape them, then
they dry off easier.
If they're in the stable
you take them back in the yard
and walk them around
until they're dry.

Different lots have different times —
one-and-a-half hours, then
it's time for the next lot.

That horse you saw yesterday,
I've backed him two or three times
and he won twice
so I won twice.
You back your horses

but that's your money
you're putting on them.

I've been grooming horses
all my life since I was a lad
and I'm twenty-six now.

I'm working in stables.
I'm up to my eyes with horses.
I'm with them all the way.

George Green

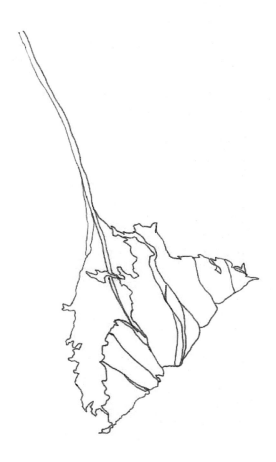

Considering The Cow

The average herd size has now increased
from about 30 cows to 130 cows.
The average yield has increased
to 1,000 gallons from about 20 gallons.
It's a good thing. Mark you,
I don't think it's a good thing
from the point of view of the cow.

The farmer doesn't get to know
the individual animal.
You get a herd of 130 cows
and the farmer would be hard-pressed
to know the name of each one.
Whereas in a herd of 30 or 40 cows
they know each one individually,
they can talk to it comfortably
in a comforting way, can't they?
They can speak to it by name.
I like to be called by my name
instead of number 13 or 14.
I think it's better
to be called by a name than a number.
It's knowing a cow's habits,
what she likes to do
and what she doesn't like to do.

I've been associated with milking-stock.
I worked for a milking machine company
and we made milking machinery.
I was considered to be
an expert in that particular field.

To personalise milking machines is impossible.
You walk into the milking parlour
and you whack on the teat-cups
regardless of the frame of mind of the cow.
But I must say milking is a combined operation,

depending on the cow and the user.
A cow needs to be comfortable in her mind
if she is to let down and release her milk.
Normally cows' udders are washed in warm water
prior to milking. This serves two purposes:
it cleans off the extraneous dung
and other matter accumulated on the teats,
and it also stimulates let-down.

They get used to it. It's the standard
of feeling with a milking machine,
it's always the same. Whereas
a man's hands vary. I would say
I used to milk four or five cows by hand
before I went to school each day.
That's before we had a milking machine.
There's a certain amount of physical pleasure involved,
but not at 5 o'clock in the morning!

We want to make the machines
as comfortable as possible
and as near hand-milking as possible.
It's useful to have a knowledge
of the hand-milking. It helped all right!

Douglas Orme

Mixing It

First I was a brickmaker,
then a baker and confectioner –
I did a bit of each.

Fisons at the brickworks –
that's a monotonous job.
We made bricks from the surrounding ground,
then along the escalator to the factory
where it was baked and pressed.
It isn't awfully interesting –
you haven't missed much,
and now the clay is gone.

I was living with my sister
next door to the bakery
and gave them a little help.
I learned how to do things.
So I became a baker.
The troughs you made the dough in
you poured in the liquid
and the salts and things mixed in.
It was the timing and all that.
I did what I was taught to do
by the baker I worked for.
The last baker's job I had
was 4 o'clock in the morning start.
Some jobs are all night –
I didn't fall for that –
that was the earliest I started
even that had been put back and back.

I started as a brickmaker
and finished as a baker
with a few changes in between.

Arthur Bye

Wheeler And Dealer

I went to school ten year
and only had one nought.
My father was a farmer
but I left the land
and went to work in a garage
repairing cars for ten year.
After that I had twenty-six weeks off
with an ulcer. When I went back
I told the boss "Only a light job."
The first he gave me was to fit
six tyres on a busette, I had
to knock 'em off by hand.
By the sixth tyre I'd collapsed on the floor.

I went to see the lady
who had the old slaughterhouse
and started on me own.
They were putting sewerage in:
"Can you keep my roadway open?"
He put planking so the cars could get across.
And he finished up lodging with us.
I was in that business ten year.
After that the land was sold.

I worked all the hours God Almighty chose to send.

While I had the garage
I went grasstrack-racing at weekend.
I started with a mini
With the name on the side 'WILD WILLY'.
I fixed the cars up after –
well it gave me something to do after tea!

Ernie Johnson

Woodwork

I'm strong on woodwork,
carpentry and woodwork —
that's my pride and joy.

I trained in nightschool,
got a living off it,
used to be in the machineshop.

I'd find out what size you wanted,
and what sort of wood you wanted,
and draw it up for you.

Did you want it painted?
Or did you want it varnished?
I'd give you a price.

If you came and it wasn't finished
or you came and it was —
two choices, aren't there?

I'm strong on woodwork.
It was a pleasure to me.
And the money!

Albert Peacock

A Lot Of Character

I'm interested in people, ordinary people,
and I feel they're neglected —
no-one seemed to write about them,
they've quite a lot of character,
some of them, so I've written
quite a few like that, on the principle
that they have the character
and I try to bring the character out.
There are some people, sophisticated people,
with no character, so I ignore them.
Human beings that have seen life —
that's what it's all about.

There's a big demand for poetry
but I didn't make a living from it.
I don't get much of a living —
I have to rely on my pension.
I'm 93, so I can't do much else!
A lot of people are interested in poetry
but they daren't let rip.
I know they get embarrassed,
but I've been here so long
there's no room for embarrassment.
You say what you've got
in your heart, and that's enough.

Fred Unwin

It Can Be Done

This is heaven
because for a lot of people it helps them.
You do it on a one-to-one
and that's right.
I feel I'm very lucky
because I've got something like poetry.

I've lots of memories, good and bad.
Most of my friends, they never say a thing —
I think they're frightened:
I've got a friend in London
and he's only phoned once in three years.

We've just come back from Madeira.
My wife noticed it and told me.
I said "I've got Alzheimers".
I could see the same signs.
He was there with his wife.
She had it. On the last three days
we stayed together,
we found a rapport.

I'm pretty healthy.
You're not in it, are you?
I was trying to look at your badge
just to make sure!

Some people can't handle it.
They think, how can they carry on?
But I don't think I want these things round my neck —
I want to live!

I'm not looking to get rid of myself,
I've never even thought of it.
I really mean it:
if you take your courage in both hands
it can be done!

Peter Van Spyk

Index of first lines

Index of titles

Other works by John Killick

Dementia-related Titles

You Are Words: Dementia Poems *Hawker, 1997*

Openings: Poems and Photographs (with Carl Cordonnier) *Hawker, 2000*

Communication and the Care of People with Dementia (with Kate Allan)
Open University Press, 2001

The Arts and Dementia Care: A Resource Guide (with Anne Davis Basting)
National Center for Creative Aging, 2003

Dementia Diary: Poetry and Prose *Hawker, 2008*

Other Titles

Poetry:
Windhorse *Rockingham, 1996*
Over the Land (with Alison McGill) *Fisherrow, 2007*

Prose:
Writing For Self-Discovery (with Myra Schneider) *Element, 1998*
Writing Your Self (with Myra Schneider) *Continuum International, 2009*

John Killick

John Killick was a teacher in further education and a prison education officer for thirty years, but a writer in his spare time. For ten years he was a small press publisher, bringing out over sixty titles. He has run many courses for writers, and co-written two texts on the subject. He has also published two books of poems.

He has worked for over fifteen years on communication with people with dementia, first of all as Writer in Residence for Westminster Health Care, and then as Research Fellow in Communication Through the Arts for Dementia Services Development Centre at the University of Stirling. As well as working in Cambridgeshire he is currently Writer in Residence for Alzheimer Scotland.

John has written extensively on the subject of Communication in Dementia, and broadcast on the BBCs Radio Three and Four and the World Service. He has given presentations and run workshops in Norway, Sweden, Denmark, Germany, Switzerland, Poland, Australia, Ireland, Canada and the USA.

Jo Chapman

Jo graduated in Embroidery/Textiles from UCE
Birmingham School of Art & Design in 1986.
She started teaching in London in 1989, where
she was associated with Goldsmiths College and
the College of North West London. From 1999
- 2002 she worked for Cambridge Regional
College as a technician, part-time lecturer and
gallery co-ordinator. From 2003 - 2005 she was
exhibitions co-ordinator at the Babylon Gallery in
Ely, and in 2004 completed an MA in Fine Art at
Norwich School of Art & Design. She became a
freelance artist and art educator in 2005.

Jo's practice is varied and her installations often
temporary. She has been making large-scale stitched wall drawings, created
on site. These cover architectural surfaces with networks of intertwined
flowers, plants and objects. Jo also works on smaller scale drawings, prints
and cut-outs. The drawings are often situated in corners, above or below eye
level. These installations draw your attention to overlooked details, highlighting
insignificant and unchampioned parts of the building. Recently she has been
working on public commissions making internal and external works in steel.

Jo has provided workshops both in galleries and in schools since 2004.
These involved general art activities with young people of all ages, and included
drawing and large scale wall pieces. She has also specialised in working adults
with learning difficulties (Wysing Arts, Cambridge 2005 and Project Artworks,
Hastings, 2007). From 2004 - 2006 Jo was a mentee for Commissions East.